# THE GREAT WESTERN MAINLINE
## A MODERN PORTRAIT

JAMIE ANDERSON

AMBERLEY

First published 2023

Amberley Publishing
The Hill, Stroud
Gloucestershire, GL5 4EP

www.amberley-books.com



ISBN 978 1 3981 1505 7 (print)
ISBN 978 1 3981 1506 4 (ebook)



British Library Cataloguing in Publication Data.
A catalogue record for this book is available from the British Library.

Origination by Amberley Publishing.
Printed in the UK.

# Introduction

The Great Western Railway came into being during 1833 and two years later the company received its Act of Incorporation from Parliament. This would allow the GWR to begin the process of constructing its railway from London Paddington to Bristol. The GWR selected a young twenty-six-year-old engineer by the name of Isambard Kingdom Brunel, who at the time was working to complete the Thames Tunnel along with his father Marc Isambard Brunel. The tunnel was the first in the world built under a navigable river.

When Brunel set to work he had the idea that passengers would be able to travel from London to the West Wales port of Neyland, where passengers would be able to board Great Western steamships heading to America. Having surveyed the route himself, Brunel chose a route that followed the Thames Valley out of London and then north of the Marlborough Downs before heading on to Bristol and Wales. The route selected was not the most popular with the board of the GWR, but Brunel chose it for its flat lay of the land that would allow much higher running speeds and faster journey times for both freight and passengers heading to and from London. The route quickly earned the nickname of Brunel's Billiards Table, and as progress on the route was made Brunel went with broad gauge track that was 7ft ¼ in wide, instead of the standard gauge width of 4ft 8 ½ in that was in use elsewhere at the time in the country.

To service and build its locomotives, the GWR needed a locomotive works and the town of Swindon was chosen. Construction of Swindon Railway Works began in 1841 and was completed in 1843. Swindon Works quickly gained a reputation for producing good, solid, reliable locos. One of the most famous steam locomotives built at Swindon was No. 3440 *City of Truro*, a member of the twenty-strong City Class locos. On 9 May 1904, *City of Truro* purportedly reached 100 mph. Other famous classes of locos followed including Castles, Halls, Grange, Manor and King class locos, with the Kings representing the pynical of GWR locomotive design. As well as the larger-tender engines the works also produced a number of tank loco classes including the iconic 1600 and 6400 class 0-6-0 pannier tanks. As well as steam power, the GWR also experimented with other types of traction. This included the GWR diesel railcars, with thirty-eight built and in service between 1934 and 1962. Steam locomotive production ended in March 1960 with the completion of 9F No. 92220 *Evening Star*. This loco was not only the last steam loco produced by the works but the last ever steam loco produced for BR.

Although steam had now ended, a new dawn was on the horizon. Diesel was coming and the works would play its part in maintaining and building the new breed of locos. Before the last steam loco rolled out of the works the works, at Swindon began building diesel-hydraulic locomotives that included thirty-eight Class 42 Warships, starting with D800 *Sir Brian Robertson* and ending with D870 *Zulu*, which were built between 1958 and 1961. The Warships were followed by the twenty-nine Class 52 Western locomotives. Locomotive production ended at Swindon with the Class 14 0-6-0s, which were built between 1964 and 1965 and numbered D9500–D95555. During 1970 Swindon works was integrated into the newly formed British Rail Engineering Ltd (BREL). The works slowly lost out as work was transferred to the other BREL sites and the end came of the once proud works on 26 March 1986.

During the 1970s British Rail was developing the next generation of high-speed trains to boost its public image and draw passengers back to the railways. This lead to the development of the Advanced Passenger Train Experimental (APT-E). This was another multiple-unit design but was powered by gas turbine engines instead of diesel engines. It made several test runs between Swindon and Reading, reaching a speed of 152.3 mph. The lessons learnt from the APT-E would be put to use with the all-electric Class 370 Advanced Passenger Train Prototype (APT-P). Though the APT program failed, it eventually gave the railways the saviour it needed in the form of the InterCity 125.

In 1994, the sector of British Rail Freight was split up into three separate companies, with the GWML mainly being served by Transrail with visits from Mainline and Loadhaul locos also happening. In 1996, the rail sector was privatised. The three freight companies, along with Rail Express Services, were bought by what was to become English Welsh & Scottish Railway (EWS), which ultimately became DB Cargo. Alongside EWS was Freightliner, founded in 1995, and these were later joined by GB Railfreight in 1999 and Colas Rail in 2006. On the passenger side of the industry, privatisation occurred in 1996, with services initially operated by Great Western Trains. This was followed by First Great Western in 1998 and, since 2015, Great Western Railway. The High Speed Train (HST) sets, later Class 43s, served until June 2019 when the new Hitachi Class 800 series of Intercity Express Trains (IET) took over from the much-loved HST sets on the long-distance routes.

The Great Western Mainline has undergone significant change since the first rails were laid in the age of Brunel. Various types of diesel-hydraulic and diesel-electric locomotives have also come and gone. With the electrification of the route west out of Paddington currently not complete to Bristol Temple Meads, the route has seen further drastic change with the Class 387 EMUs cascading the older DMUs onto secondary routes and the IET fleet taking over from the HST fleet on the long-distance routes. The current scene, although not as varied as it once was, still has plenty to offer the rail enthusiast.

**1 June 2019**

GWR Class 43 No. 002 *Sir Kenneth Grange* is seen at Paddington working the Flying Banana railtour along with classmate 43198. This was the last ever GWR HST working on the Great Western Mainline before the new Hitachi 800 series of units took over from these much-loved workhorses.

**1 June 2019**

GWR Class 43 No. 198 *Driver Stan Martin 25 June 1950–6 November 2004/Driver Brian Cooper 15 June 1947–5 October 1999*. Sits under the roof at Paddington along with classmate 43002 with the Flying Banana railtour. The tour was a final farewell to the HST sets and worked along the routes the class were synonymous with.

**17 July 2021**

DRS Class 57 No. 310 *Pride of Cumbria* rests at the buffer stops at Paddington having brought in the previous night's Night Riviera sleeper service from Penzance. GWR has had to hire-in DRS Class 57s due to issues surrounding their own 57/6 fleet.

**2 June 2022**

GWR Class 57 No. 603 *Tintagel Castle* is seen on a bright sunny morning at Paddington having brought in the previous night's Night Riviera sleeper service. GWR have had good use out of their 57s but recently confirmed they will be replaced in the future. Note the height of the cast numberplate on the side of 603.

**16 July 2022**

GWR Class 57 No. 605 *Totnes Castle* sits at the buffer stops at Paddington having brought in the previous night's sleeper service from Penzance. All of the GWR 57 fleet are named after castles and carry this livery, with the exception of 57604.

**5 September 2021**

GBRF Class 69 No. 001 *Mayflower* sits along with classmate 69002 at Paddington after bringing in the final leg of the four-day GBRF 2021 This Time it's Personal railtour. This was the first major appearance of the Class 69s on the rail network.

**5 September 2021**

GBRF Class 69 No. 002 *Bob Tiller CM&EE* along with classmate 69001 rests under the roof at Paddington at the end of the four-day GBRF 2021 railtour. The 69s are rebuilt locomotives: a Class 56 body with the engine cab layout and other components from a Class 66.

**26 August 2019**

Heathrow Express Class 332 No. 013 rests at Paddington with a classmate before another load of holidaymakers board to start their journey to Heathrow. At this point the 332 fleet had just over a year remaining before scrapping.

**2 June 2022**

GWR Class 387 No. 167 waits for any late-running passengers at Paddington before it heads off with a service to Newbury on a fine sunny afternoon.

**16 October 2021**

Heathrow Express Class 387 No. 136 waits time for its next working to Heathrow along with classmate 387135. The Class 387s replaced the Class 332s on the airport workings in December 2020 and, along with a new livery, underwent modifications to make them suitable for their new role.

**2 June 2022**
Heathrow Express Class 387 No. 130, along with an unidentified classmate, has just pulled into Paddington with passengers that have just arrived in the UK. The Heathrow Express 387s had been named earlier in the year. 130 carries the name *San Francisco*.

**2 June 2022**
Heathrow Express Class 387 No. 139 *Dublin* waits to depart Paddington with an unidentified classmate on the platinum jubilee long weekend with passengers heading to Heathrow. This view shows how the platform ends are curved at Paddington.

**2 June 2022**

GWR Class 800 No. 003 *Queen Victoria/Queen Elizabeth II* is seen at Paddington as it prepares for its next working to the west. Fittingly, 003 carries the name and on this date the official emblem for Queen Elizabeth's platinum jubilee, which celebrated her seventy years on the throne.

**2 June 2022**

GWR Class 800 No. 033 *Martin Heath* is seen having just arrived at London Paddington from the West Country as the GWR staff prepare the IET for its next working. Here, No. 033 has had the coupler covers retracted and the coupler unit extended.

**2 June 2022**

GWR Class 800 No. 035 *Naomi Betts* is seen under the enormous glass roof of Paddington as it prepares for its next westbound departure away from the capital.

**2 June 2022**

GWR Class 800 No. 304 is seen at Paddington having just arrived with a full load of passengers heading into London for the jubilee celebrations. 304 is sharing platform space with one of the Heathrow Express Class 387s in this shot.

**2 June 2022**

GWR Class 802 No. 008 *Rick Rescorla* is seen at platform one at Paddington as it awaits it's next departure. 008 would appear to have had a new coupling cover fitted while at North Pole Depot. Look at the difference between the yellow of the cover and the yellow of the bodyshell.

**2 June 2022**

GWR Class 802 No. 018 *Jeremy Doyle* is seen at Paddington being prepared for its next departure. The IET fleet has really changed things on the GWML – they are quicker off the mark than the HST sets, cutting journey times on the route.

**22 June 2019**

TFL Rail Class 345 No. 003 arrives at Ealing Broadway on a glorious summer day as it takes passengers towards the capital. These electric multiple units will serve the Elizabeth line.

**22 June 2019**

TFL Rail Class 360 No. 204 makes a stop at Ealing Broadway while working a Heathrow Connect service back to Paddington. The Heathrow Connect services were absorbed into TFL Rail in May 2018 to form part of the Elizabeth line services. The fleet of 360/2 EMUs were withdrawn by September 2020 and purchased by Rail Operations Group in 2021.

**22 June 2019**

GWR Class 387 No. 157 is seen with an unidentified classmate at Ealing Broadway on a local stopping service heading into London Paddington. The Class 387s replaced the Class 165 and 166 diesel multiple units on the local stopping services, sending the DMUs further west.

**22 June 2019**

Metropolitan Railway Electric Locomotive No. 12 *Sarah Siddons* is seen at Ealing Broadway on the Underground lines working the Steam on the Underground District 150 celebrations, along with steam locomotive Metropolitan E Class No. 1. Built between 1922 and 1923, a total of twenty electric locos were built, with only Nos 5 and 12 surviving.

**31 August 2020**

Scottish Thirty-Seven Group Class 37 No. 025 *Inverness TMD* is seen at Reading waiting for the signal to proceed with a test train. Of note is the Highland Rail transfer underneath the leading cab window.

**22 September 2022**

GBRF Class 47 No. 727 *Edinburgh Castle/Caisteal Dhun Eideann* is seen at Reading getting underway with a late-running unit drag, in this case with an EMR Class 360 No. 110 that is heading for work at Eastleigh Arlington Works.

**19 July 2017**

Freightliner Class 66 No. 585 comes to a stop at Reading for a crew change with a long rake of loaded intermodal wagons heading towards London, with a possible destination of London Gateway or Felixstowe intermodal terminals.

**19 July 2017**

Freightliner Class 66 No. 591 is seen later in the day during a crew change at Reading with a long rake of intermodal wagons that are heading west. The train will either go via Oxford or run down the Great Western Mainline towards Bristol.

**1 December 2022**

Freightliner Class 66 No. 537 is seen making a crew change at Reading with the 6Z86 diagram working from West Drayton Frays Sidings to East Usk Yard with a long rake of box wagons loaded with aggregate in tow.

**3 January 2022**

GWR Class 165 No. 106 is seen at Reading awaiting departure time with a stopping service to Redhill. These diesel multiple units were a common sight on services at Reading until the introduction of the Class 387s. Nowadays the 165 and 166 fleets only work to either Redhill or Basingstoke.

**3 January 2022**

GWR Class 165 No. 107 is seen at the other end of Reading station waiting departure time with a stopping service to Basingstoke. This non-electrified route is likely to be turned over to the Class 769 multiple units when they enter service.

**3 January 2022**

CrossCountry Class 220 No. 021 is seen at Reading making a station stop while working in multiple with classmate 220013 at the other end. CrossCountry use these diesel multiple units on their long-distance services along with the Class 221 and Class 43 HST sets.

**1 December 2022**

CrossCountry Class 220 No. 015 ticks over under the main walkway at Reading along with an unidentified Class 221 Super Voyager as the pairing prepare to head off on the next leg of their journey.

**3 January 2022**

CrossCountry Class 221 No. 135 is seen pausing at Reading to pick up passengers. The Class 221s are identical to the Class 220s, with the only difference being the inclusion of an extra car to make them into a five-car unit.

**3 January 2022**

TFL Rail Class 345 No. 055 is about to depart from Reading with a service to Paddington. This view really shows off the striking livery of the Class 345. The Class 345s started operating from Reading during December 2019.

**22 April 2022**

TFL Rail Class 345 No. 059 is seen at Reading awaiting departure time with a service to London Paddington. The Elizabeth line was officially opened by the Queen on 17 May 2022. The line allows passengers to travel from Reading to Shenfield.

**1 December 2022**

TFL Rail Class 345 No. 032 is seen at Reading with an Elizabeth line service. The line can take passengers all the way from Reading, under Central London, then through to Abbey Wood, or by changing services at Paddington they can head to Shenfield.

**3 January 2022**

GWR Class 387 No. 149 awaits departure time with a stopping service to Newbury – a journey of some 17 miles and six chains. The route will take 149 past Reading West, where it then runs via Theale and Thatcham before arriving at journey's end.

**1 December 2022**

GWR Class 387 No. 173 sits at Reading with an unidentified classmate as the pair form an eight-car working preparing to depart for Didcot Parkway with a stopping service.

**3 January 2022**

c2c Class 387 No. 301 prepares to work a stopping service to Newbury. GWR has hired three c2c 387s for a one-year period to cover for GWR 387s that are having to cover Class 800 series IET diagrams due to cracks being found on the GWR IET lifting points.

**27 January 2018**

SWR Class 450 No. 546, along with classmate 450 017, are seen at Reading on a damp wet day working the 12:12 service stopping to London Waterloo. Of note is that 546 still carries the livery and branding of SouthWest Trains.

**3 January 2022**

SWR Class 450 No. 126 still in it's SWT livery but with SWR branding along with classmate 450 096, which carries full SWR livery and branding. 126 prepares to depart Reading for Waterloo with an afternoon stopping service.

**22 April 2022**

SWR Class 450 No. 056 is seen at Reading in full South Western Railway livery along with an unidentified classmate. The pair will form a stopping service that will terminate at London Waterloo.

**1 December 2022**

SWR Class 450 No. 009 brings a dash of color to a grey foggy day along with its classmate and sister unit 450008. The pair are being prepared to head out on a stopping service to London Waterloo.

**31 August 2020**

SWR Class 458 No. 507 along with classmate 458 529 are seen at Reading preparing to depart with the hourly stopping service to London Waterloo. Once again, 507 still carries the old SWT livery.

**3 January 2022**

SWR Class 458 No. 532 is seen at Reading preparing to depart for Waterloo along with classmate 458 513. The days of the 450s and 458s on the Reading–Waterloo line could be numbered due to the planned introduction of the new Class 701s.

**22 September 2022**

GWR Class 769 No. 935 is about to depart from Reading heading possibly to Redhill with a mileage accumulation run. This test also allowed the crew to run on both the third rail system and the unit's diesel engines.

**22 September 2022**

GWR Class 800 No. 012 is seen at Reading trailing an unidentified classmate as the pair pick up passengers and head west along the Great Western Mainline. This view shows the height difference of the two running lines at this location.

**1 December 2022**

GWR Class 800 No. 005 heads west out of Reading into the enveloping fog that has covered most of the Great Western Mainline, along with an unidentified classmate.

**31 August 2020**

GWR Class 800 No. 313 stops at Reading on a working to London Paddington. The 800 series replaced the Class 43 HST sets on these long-distance workings. The Class 800/3 are nine-car BI-MODE sets that can run on either 25Kv AC overhead lines or by diesel engines.

**3 January 2022**

GWR Class 802 No. 014 is seen at Reading heading west from the capital a few days into the new year. The Class 802/0 are five-car BI-MODE sets and are very similar to the 800 series IETs. The GWR Class 802s have had modifications to their roof-mounted brake resistors so they can work along the Dawlish sea wall.

**1 December 2022**

GWR Class 802 No. 008 *RNLB Solomon Browne* is seen having just arrived at Reading while heading west with an unidentified classmate on a very foggy afternoon. RNLB *Solomon Browne* was a lifeboat that was lost on the night of 19 December 1981 while coming to the aid of *Union Star*. Sadly all eight crew onboard *Solomon Browne* and all those onboard *Union Star* perished in what became known as the Penlee lifeboat disaster.

**3 January 2022**

Rail Grinding Train No. DR 79304 makes for an interesting sight at Reading as it reverses while working the 401A Reading triangle sidings to York skeleton OTM sidings on what could have been its first working of the new year.

**8 September 2022**

Colas Rail Class 37 No. 219 *Jonty Jarvis 8-12-1998 to 18-3-2005* is seen at Didcot ticking over on the rear of a test train that has just reversed and is about to head back to Derby. Classmate 37421 is at the other end.

**8 September 2022**

Colas Rail Class 37 No. 421 is seen awaiting for the signal to proceed at Didcot, where it will then head back to Derby with classmate 37219 at the other end. Of note is the two PLPR (Plain Line Pattern Recognition) coaches in the middle of the test train. These record and detect any defects such as damaged sleepers or missing rail clips.

**22 April 2022**

Hanson & Hall Class 50 No. 008 *Thunderer* and GBRF Class 50 No. 007 *Hercules* are seen at Didcot Parkway working double-headed on the Branch Line Society railtour The Honeybourne Hoover. This ran from Burton-on-Trent to Eastleigh.

**8 September 2022**

DB Cargo Class 60 No. 059 *Swinden Dalesman* is seen about to get on the move heading west from Didcot with a long rake of tank wagons working from Theale Puma along the GWML to its destination at Robeston sidings in South Wales.

**5 May 2018**

DB Cargo Class 66 No. 130 is seen next to Didcot Parkway in the stabling points and has classmate 66078 for company while awaiting its next turn of duty. The stabling points here are normally occupied by a Class 66, although others can turn up from time to time.

**3 January 2022**

DB Cargo Class 66 No. 025 is found a few days into the new year in the stabling point at Didcot Parkway. 025 still wears its previous owner's livery and branding of English, Welsh & Scottish Railways (EWS).

**22 April 2022**

DB Cargo Class 66 No. 142 *Maritime Intermodal Three* is seen at Didcot Parkway awaiting its next duty. DB Cargo has a fleet of seven 66s in this livery, which was to celebrate the partnership that DB has with Maritime Transport.

**8 September 2022**

DB Cargo Class 66 No. 070 is seen getting underway once more after a crew change at Didcot. It has a rake of car transporter wagons that are conveying new BMW Minis from the plant at Morris Cowley for shipment abroad via Southhampton Eastern Docks. These wagons are used solely on the BMW Mini workings.

**8 September 2022**

GBRF Class 66 No. 730 *Whitemoor* is seen at Didcot slowing for a change of crew on a rather wet and cloudy day while working an intermodal service from Southampton West Docks to East Midlands Gateway Terminal.

**1 December 2022**

GBRF Class 66 No. 775 *HMS Argyll* is about to get underway once more after a crew change at Didcot Parkway while hauling a rake of intermodal wagons from Southampton West Docks through to East Midlands Gateway intermodal terminal.

**8 September 2022**

Colas Rail Class 70 No. 801 crawls slowly into Didcot for a quick crew change with a loaded rake of engineering wagons full of ballast. Journey's end is not far as the loco is working from Eastleigh East Yard to Hinksey Sidings, which is just a little further up the track.

**5 May 2018**

GWR Class 165 No. 123 has just arrived at Didcot Parkway with a local service from Oxford. The local service from Oxford is still firmly in the hands of the 165s, however should the overhead wires be extended to Oxford this could result in a change of traction.

**5 May 2018**

GWR Class 387 No. 133 awaits departure time with a service towards the capital working in multiple with classmate 387 137. The 387s work the long-distance stopping services from Didcot via Reading through to London Paddington.

**2 April 2022**

GWR Class 387 No. 155 is seen at Didcot Parkway with an unidentified classmate as they prepare for a working towards London Paddington on a cloudy afternoon.

**8 September 2022**

GWR Class 387 No. 144 hums quietly away along with an unidentified classmate at Didcot Parkway as they await their next working with a stopping service to the capital.

**1 December 2022**

GWR Class 387 No. 146 is seen with an unidentified classmate at Didcot Parkway as the pair prepare to work a stopping service through to London Paddington.

**1 December 2022**

GWR Class 387 No. 166 is seen waiting along with classmate 387 151 at Didcot Parkway while working an empty unit move. The 387s will proceed out to Didcot West End, where the EMUs will reverse and come back into platform four.

**8 September 2022**

GWR Class 800 No. 018 is seen at Didcot Parkway getting a good soaking along with classmate 800008, which carries rainbow pride detailing as they work west from London Paddington.

**22 April 2022**

GWR Class 800 No. 315 gets underway from Didcot Parkway with a service heading towards the west. This view really shows off the sleek lines that characterise the IET fleet and the nose cone that opens for when the coupler is required.

**8 September 2022**

GWR Class 800 No. 317 *Freya Bevan* is seen at Didcot Parkway in the pouring rain as it picks up passengers while heading west along the Great Western Mainline. It is midday and the station appears almost empty.

**1 December 2022**

GWR Class 802 No. 113 is seen at Didcot Parkway about to depart with the 1C17 diagram, which is running from London Paddington to Bristol Temple Meads.

**6 August 2022**

WCRC Class 33 Nos 025 and 029 are seen getting underway from Swindon while working the Pathfinder Tours Dorset Coast Explorer railtour, which started at Burton-On-Trent and is heading to the seaside resort of Weymouth on a perfect summer morning.

**15 March 2022**

Rail Operations Group Class 37 No. 884 *Cepheus* powers through Swindon under a lightly clouded sky as it drags a Class 365 electric multiple unit on its final journey to be broken up for scrap in South Wales.

**22 March 2022**

Rail Operations Group Class 37 No. 800 *Cassiopeia* is on the unit drag duty this time around as it charges through Swindon hauling a Transport for London Class 317 EMU on its final journey to South Wales for scrapping.

**29 October 2022**

West Coast Railway Company Class 37 No. 668 is seen at Swindon on a cloudy damp morning while working Pathfinder Tours' The Cotswold Caper along with classmate 37676, out of sight at the rear.

**29 October 2022**

West Coast Railway Company Class 37 No. 676 *Loch Rannoch* is seen on the rear of Pathfinder Tours' The Cotswold Caper railtour, with classmate 37668 on the front. The 37s are about to depart and head up the South Marston Euro Terminal freight branch line before heading to Burton-On-Trent, where the tour started that morning.

**12 May 2021**

LSL Blue Pullman Class 43s Nos 046 *Geoff Drury 1930–1999 Steam Preservation and Computerised Track Recording Pioneer* and 055 are seen in the fading light at Swindon working the return leg of the Settle & Carlisle Pullman railtour. 055 is just out of sight at the other end of the formation.

**12 May 2021**

LSL Class 43 No. 055 heads off into the setting sun at Swindon while working the Settle & Carlisle Pullman Railtour with classmate 43046 at the other end of the HST formation.

**3 August 2021**

Network Rail Class 43s Nos 299 and 290 are seen at Swindon coming to a halt while working a test train. It is worth noting that both 43s are still in their LNER liveries and carry Network Rail branding. The red of the locos and yellow of the coaches make for a colorful sight.

**24 March 2022**

Colas Rail Class 43 No. 272 is seen at Swindon working a test train with 43274, which can be seen in the next photo. 272 is another of the ex-LNER 43s and still retains its previous livery, but with Colas Rail branding.

**24 March 2022**

Colas Rail Class 43 No. 274 stops at Swindon while on a test train diagram along with 43272, as seen in the previous photo. 274 is one of the ex-East Midlands Railway 43s and still displays that livery but again carries Colas Rail branding.

**26 March 2022**

GBRF Class 50s Nos 007 *Hercules* and 049 *Defiance* are seen at Swindon having just dropped off passengers while working the Springtime Hoovering in Devon railtour. The highlight of this tour was traversing the recently reopened branch line to Okehampton.

**20 October 2022**

Colas Rail Class 56 No. 090 is seen having just come off the Golden Valley line with classmate 56113 at the rear of the Cheltenham Lansdown loop to Swindon Transfer RHTT diagram. As the pair wait to cross over the running lines to access Swindon Transfer the build up of grime on 090 is obvious – the side of the loco is almost uniformly brown.

**25 October 2022**

Colas Rail Class 56 No. 096 is seen at Swindon with classmate 56113 on the rear as they wait for the signal to proceed into Swindon Transfer with the daily RHTT diagram from Cheltenham Lansdown loop. Colas are alternating the Class 56s on this working; 096 looks pretty clean compared to 56113, as seen in the next image.

**25 October 2022**

Colas Rail Class 56 No. 113 is seen at the rear of the same RHTT working in the previous image with classmate 56096 on the front. 56113 has been the regular grid on this season's workings so far, as shown by the grime build up on the loco's sides.

**23 March 2022**

DC Rail Freight Class 56 No. 091 *Driver Wayne Gaskell The Godfather* is seen at Swindon as it prepares to head back towards Oxford on a driver route learning run in preparation for a new freight working.

**28 June 2021**

Freightliner Class 59 No. 004 *PAUL A HAMMOND* in Aggregate Industry livery pulls out of Swindon East loop having run round its rake of stone wagons and into the station with the weekday aggregate working from Merehead Quarry to Wootton Bassett F.Y.

**17 March 2021**

Freightliner Class 59 No. 101 *Village of Whatley*, in Hason livery, is seen at a railway overbridge just down the mainline from Swindon station. 101 has just uncoupled from its stone train and is in the process of running round to the other end of the wagons before it heads past Swindon station.

**16 June 2020**

DB Cargo Class 59 No. 202 *Alan Meddows Taylor MD Mendip Rail Limitied* pulls out of Swindon East loop with a rake of loaded stone hoppers on a sunny afternoon as it heads towards Wotton Bassett for unloading.

**23 March 2021**

Freightliner Class 59 No. 205 is seen at the railway overbridge not far from Swindon station as it runs round its rake of stone wagons. Freightliner brought DB Cargo's fleet of 59s and, as we can see here, 205 is still in its previous DB red livery but minus the DB branding.

**15 March 2022**

Freightliner Class 59 No. 206 *John F. Yeoman Rail Pioneer* comes to a stop at Swindon waiting for the signal to proceed into Swindon East loop. This is what the ex-DB Cargo 59s will look like when they have been re-liveried into the new Freightliner orange, black and yellow livery.

**11 August 2018**

DB Cargo Class 60 No. 020 *The Willows* rumbles through Swindon on a sunny summer afternoon with the Saturday's only fuel tanker train working from Theale to the oil terminal at Westerleigh.

**17 August 2021**

DB Cargo Class 60 No. 092 is seen at Swindon waiting departure time having shunted its rake of steel wagons at the Hawksworth steel terminal. The line on which 092 is resting is not electrified and is used solely by locomotives visiting the steel terminal.

**15 March 2022**

DB Cargo Class 60 No. 066 is seen at Swindon as it performs the various shunting moves with its rake of steel wagons while they are loaded at the Hawksworth steel terminal. The tug has just set back as it moves along round the back of platform one to collect its wagons.

**15 March 2022**

DB Cargo Class 60 No. 066. Having completed its various manoeuvres, 066 is now seen awaiting departure time with its rake of steel wagons. This particular Class 60 displays the advertising livery for Drax, which owns and operates the Drax biomass power station.

**31 August 2022**

DCRail Class 60 No. 046 *William Wilberforce* passes through Swindon with a rake of empty stone wagons heading to Machen Quarry, where it will be loaded up. This is a new diagram and DCRail use either Class 56 or Class 60 locos as haulage.

**25 October 2022**

DCRail Class 60 No. 028 charges through Swindon with a rake of loaded stone wagons, heading east. The blue advertising livery for Cappagh and the matching wagons bring a dash of colour to this picture.

**22 March 2022**

Colas Rail Class 66 No. 846 charges through Swindon under threatening skies with a rake of engineering wagons, heading east. The Colas 66s are a rare sight at Swindon, this being only the third time I had seen them.

**20 October 2022**

Colas Rail Class 66 No. 850 *David Maidment OBE* is seen at Swindon, working the Hereford to Swindon Transfer RHTT diagram along with stand-in Freightliner Class 66554, which replaced a failed Colas 66 classmate. After only a few trips, 850 is starting to get a bit filthy from the leaf-busting work.

**24 April 2017**

DB Cargo Class 66 No. 066 *Geoff Spencer* is seen at Swindon awaiting its next turn of duty. This photo was taken before electrification arrived on this part of the GWML. Also note how clean 066 is, possibly being an ex-works loco.

**20 May 2017**

DB Cargo Class 66 No. 171 stops at Swindon platform three with an engineering working consisting of ballast wagons. Very shortly this view would change forever when the electrification project reached Swindon and the wires went up.

**8 June 2019**

DB Cargo Class 66 No. 128 is seen ticking over at Swindon while waiting for the signal to proceed as it hauls a rake of very old wagons to Didcot yard. 128 looks very smart in this picture, having just been cleaned.

**22 March 2021**

DB Cargo Class 66 No. 111 is seen reversing out on to the Great Western Mainline just east of Swindon station, coming from the short European Metal Recycling freight-only line with a loaded rake of scrap wagons. This view gives an idea of just how curved the line into the facility is.

**28 June 2021**

DB Cargo Class 66 No. 131 accelerates hard past platform one at Swindon with a hint of clag while hauling the Monday to Saturday Northolt sidings to Severnside Sita empty binliner diagram. The loaded working runs late at night to the waste terminal, which is situated on the freight-only Brentford Goods branch line.

**26 March 2022**

DB Cargo Class 66s Nos 169 and 104 are bathed in early morning spring sunshine at Swindon as they get underway once more, double-headed with a long heavy rake of wagons. This view shows the contrast in livery of ex-EWS 169 and the DB Cargo red of 104.

**31 August 2022**

DB Cargo Class 66 No. 136 has just pulled out of Swindon East loop and into the station with the weekday binliner working, heading west. 136 was the first freight loco to haul the first part of the first London UK to Yiwu China freight train, as shown by the vinyl stickers it is adorned with.

**13 April 2019**

Freightliner Class 66 No. 512 sits in the centre track at Swindon on a chilly spring morning with a well loaded westbound intermodal working waiting for the signal to proceed. The destination is most likely the Bristol Railport freightliner terminal.

**25 March 2021**

Freightliner Class 66 No. 501 *Japan 2001* runs round its stone train that is heading to the offloading point at Wotton Bassett. Although normally a Class 59 diagram, on this occasion a Class 66 is in charge.

**28 June 2021**

Freightliner Class 66 No. 536 waits for the signal to proceed at Swindon with a rake of loaded rail sleeper wagons that are heading east. The Class 66 will get the track after the GWR IET on platform three has departed.

**22 March 2022**

Freightliner Class 66 No. 554 comes to a stop at Swindon on a light engine move while dragging classmate 66594 *NYK Spirit of Kyoto*. This is often how locos move between locations and depots.

**24 March 2022**

Freightliner Class 66 No. 563 ticks over on the centre line at Swindon waiting for the signal to proceed as it heads east with a well-loaded intermodal service on a warm spring afternoon.

**20 October 2022**

Freightliner Class 66 No. 554 is seen on the Up mainline along with Colas Rail Class 66850 while working the seasonal RHTT (Rail Head Treatment Train) diagram from Hereford to Swindon Transfer. 554 was brought in to cover for the failure of the booked Colas Class 66 and after arriving at Swindon Transfer departed west.

**22 March 2022**

Freightliner Class 66 No. 601 *The Hope Valley* races through Swindon with a rake of aggregate wagons while working the Hayes & Harlington tarmac sidings to East Usk yard diagram. This working is always in the hands of a Class 66 and tends to yield a 66/6, as seen here.

**18 July 2019**

Freightliner Class 66 No. 623 powers through Swindon on a fine sunny day with a short rake of railway sleepers. 623 has just been turned out in the Freightliner orange and black livery. This was one of the first Freightliner 66s to receive this livery.

**17 March 2021**

GBRF Class 66 No. 721 *Harry Beck* passes the overbridge just before Swindon station with a rake of aggregate wagons. 721 carries a one-a-kind livery that shows the London Underground map designed by Harry Beck, which is still in use today.

**28 June 2021**

GBRF Class 66 No. 724 *Drax Power Station* is going full speed as it passes through Swindon while dragging another unfortunate London Overground electric multiple unit to its ultimate demise in South Wales. The wagon behind the 66 is a barrier wagon, which is used when two different types of coupling are used that would be incompatible.

**15 March 2022**

GBRF Class 66 No. 761 *Wensleydale Railway Association 25 Years 1990–2015* races past platform four at Swindon with a rake of vans that are loaded with finished steel products. In the background, DB Cargo 60066 can be seen shunting its rake of steel wagons.

**15 March 2022**

GBRF Class 66 No. 781 heads east through Swindon with a short rake of empty wagons with a working for the Ministry of Defence. These MOD workings are irregular and can vary from just a few wagons to a long rake of wagons carrying armoured vehicles.

**27 December 2021**

GBRF Class 66 No. 770 stops at platform four at Swindon with a rake of cement tanks while working the 6V84 Clitheroe Castle Cement–Avonmouth Hanson sidings. The sun is just setting after a day of rain, which adds to this picture's atmosphere.

**31 August 2022**

GBRF Class 66 No. 722 *Sir Edward Watkin* has the centre line as it passes through Swindon at pace with a Ministry of Defence working consisting of seven wagons heading from Marchwood MOD to Kineton MOD.

**20 October 2022**

GBRF Class 66 No. 758 *The Pavior* has just been given the green signal and is about to pull out of Swindon with a rake of wagons from storage at Long Marston GBRF. Having come down the Golden Valley line, 758 will head along the GWML to Willeseden Euroterminal GBRF.

**20 May 2018**

Colas Rail Class 70s Nos 812, 803, 814 and 807 rumble through Swindon on a cloudy Sunday afternoon heading east in a light engine convoy move that had likely started at Westbury, where a large number of 70s from Colas are normally found.

**22 March 2022**

Colas Rail Class 70 No. 817 makes a rare appearance at Swindon stopped on the centre line on a red signal with a long rake of engineering wagons that are used for taking away or carrying materials to the engineering site. Class 70s are occasionally seen at Swindon but rarely in daylight hours, often moving under the cover of darkness.

**5 May 2018**

GWR Class 150 No. 216 sits at Swindon platform two as it prepares to depart with a local stopping service to Westbury. The masts for the electrification are now up but are without the various wire supports and the wires themselves.

**22 September 2018**

GWR Class 150 No. 261 is seen at Swindon on platform two in an almost identical shot as its classmate in the previous photo. 261 is once again waiting to depart with a local stopping service and progress on the electrification can be clearly seen as the wires and the wire supports are now up.

**11 August 2018**

GWR Class 158 No. 951 basks in the sun on a beautiful summer day at Swindon as it awaits departure time with a local stopping service to either Westbury or Gloucester. With the introduction of the Class 387s, these units were replaced by cascaded 165 and 166 DMUs.

**12 May 2021**

GWR Class 158 No. 957 rests at Swindon between duties as it awaits departure time with a local stopping service on a fine spring evening. In the background the listed building of Swindon's station can be seen.

**9 December 2022**

GWR Class 158 No. 766 sits in the last rays of winter sun at Swindon as it awaits departure time with a stopping service to Westbury.

**9 July 2018**

SWR Class 158 No. 888 makes for an interesting appearance at Swindon while working one of the weekday stopping services to Gloucester. For a while GWR had to hire in SWR 158s to cover for a shortage of their own DMUs that were available on the route.

**4 August 2018**

GWR Class 165 No. 132 is seen at Swindon awaiting its next turn of duty on a local stopping service. When the Class 387s entered service, the class 165 and 166 DMUs were cascaded west – one such diagram they took over was the local services out of Swindon.

**15 April 2021**

GWR Class 165 No. 133 prepares to depart with another local stopping service from Swindon on a warm sunny day. The 165 and 166 fleets can now be seen on local services all over the western end of the GWML, being concentrated around Bristol.

**31 August 2022**

Transport For Wales Class 231 No. 011 is seen at Swindon while on mileage accumulation runs between Cardiff and Swindon prior to entering service in the future. The Class 231 is among several new types on order for TFW for a massive fleet renewal.

**22 May 2021**

GWR Class 387 No. 147 is seen at Swindon with classmate 387 151 as they prepare to depart for the capital. This was a period of great concern for GWR as the IET fleet had been withdrawn a few weeks earlier due to cracks found on the welds of the lifting points, forcing GWR to use 387s on IET diagrams.

**22 May 2021**

GWR Class 387 No. 164 is covering another IET diagram along with classmate 387 169, heading once again for London Paddington. The withdrawal of the IET fleet caused gaps that needed to be filled so GWR hired in a number of 387s from both c2c and Gatwick Express.

**29 May 2021**

GWR Class 387 No. 170 along with an unidentified classmate bask in the sun at Swindon as they await departure time with a service to London Paddington while covering another IET diagram as that fleet was being inspected for cracks on the lifting point welds.

**10 May 2021**

GWR Class 769 No. 943 has just arrived at Swindon platform one with a test run from Reading and is preparing to head back once the signal changes and the crew have carried out checks on the unit. The Class 769s are rebuilt from older Class 319s – GWR has nineteen of these tri-mode multiple units on order.

**29 May 2021**

GWR Class 800 No. 025 *Captain Sir Tom Moore*, along with classmate 800026, is seen at Swindon as they await departure time with a westbound service on a rather dark and cloudy day.

**23 March 2022**

GWR Class 800 No. 022 *Tulbahadur Pun VC* pauses at Swindon on a bright sunny day while working east towards the capital with an unidentified classmate. With ten carriages between them you can see why platforms at some stations had to be lengthened.

**9 December 2022**

GWR Class 800 No. 021 has dropped the pantograph and started up the diesel engines as it prepares to head up the Golden Valley line with a service for Cheltenham Spa. Both five- and nine-car IET sets ply this route.

**28 June 2021**

GWR Class 800 No. 306 *Allan Leonard Lewis VC / Harold Day DSC* has just arrived at Swindon with a London-bound service. 306 is a tribute IET adorned with poppies and the names, photos and stories of the GWR staff who died during the First World War.

**15 March 2022**

GWR Class 800 No. 321 gets a soaking as it is caught in a downpour at Swindon while working an eastbound service towards Paddington. In this photograph 321 is wearing its face mask, which was applied at the start of the Covid-19 pandemic to remind customers to wear a mask on public transport.

**22 March 2022**

GWR Class 800 No. 315 catches the sun at Swindon as it prepares to depart west with a service to either Bristol or South Wales. In this view on the office block's back corner, the old British Rail double-arrow symbol can be seen.

**9 December 2022**

GWR Class 800 No. 307 is caught in the setting sun on a cold, frosty winter day at Swindon as it heads east towards the capital. The passengers will surely be thankful for a warm, climate-controlled IET.

**9 December 2022**

GWR Class 800 No. 320 is about to head off into the setting sun with the driver having the sun visor pulled down.

**29 May 2021**

GWR Class 802 No. 007 pauses at Swindon as it heads west from London Paddington just as another IET arrives heading in the opposite direction Note the length of scrap rail in the gap between the tracks on the centre line.

**29 May 2021**

GWR Class 802 No. 020 is about to depart from platform four at Swindon heading west from the capital. 020 carries a unique livery on its end driving carriages, which is a tribute to all the key workers during the Covid-19 pandemic.

**22 March 2022**

GWR Class 802 No. 103 looks very clean and tidy having been through the cleaning area at North Pole Depot, which is where the IET fleet is maintained by Hitachi for GWR. The depot is not far from Paddington. 103 is about to set off once again, heading west from Swindon.

**9 July 2018**

Network Rail Class 950 No. 001 makes a rare appearance at Swindon, where the crew is preparing to head west. This DMU does the same job as the new measurement train but is used on branch lines where there are restrictions. 950001 is a purpose track-monitoring unit based on a Class 150 DMU.

**25 October 2022**

Network Rail Class 950 No. 001 is once again seen at Swindon, this time performing a reversing movement at platform two having worked in from the Bristol area. This view gives a good glimpse of the extra lights installed for when work is carried out in darkness.

**17 April 2017**

Network Rail Electrification Vehicle No. DR 76905 sits at the head of a lengthy number of stabled classmates in the Swindon electrification depot over the Easter period. Note the stacks of piling tubes, which when in position will support the OHLE equipment.

**11 August 2018**

Network Rail Electrification Vehicle No. 76932 *GAVIN ROBERTS* passes through Swindon heading west with classmates DR 76922 and DR 76903. The electrification depot is located just east of Swindon station and can be seen from a passing train or from the nearby overbridge.

**15 March 2022**

Network Rail Electrification Vehicles Nos DR 76911 and DR 76913 are seen at Swindon on the centre track being held at a red signal. These two vehicles are not far from home now and will proceed past the depot and reverse into Swindon East loop to get access to the depot. This fleet of vehicles were built especially for the electrification of the GWML and have different modules for a variety of tasks.

**11 August 2018**

Colas Rail Tamper No. DR 73924 makes use of the quieter railway at the weekend as it races through Swindon at full speed on the centre track, heading to its next job site. Note how compact 73924 is compared to 73935 in the following image.

**15 March 2022**

Colas Rail Tamper No. DR 73935 is seen waiting for the signal to proceed at Swindon's platform one on a rather cloudy day, with the threat of rain never being too far away.

**22 March 2022**

Colas Rail Tamper No. DR 73905 is seen at Swindon being held by a red signal at it waits to depart eastward on a fine sunny morning. The tamping equipment can be seen on the other half of 73905 about halfway along its body.

**24 March 2022**

Network Rail Stoneblower No. DR 80211 is held at a red signal at Swindon while heading east towards its next job. This view gives a great shot of the crane that is used to load the hopper that is behind the cab, which at this moment is covered.

**30 November 2022**

DB Cargo Class 67 No. 007 is seen pulling out of Bath Spa with a rake of empty Pullman coaches that are being taken for servicing before the return working to London Victoria. 007 was given a special livery for the platinum jubilee of Queen Elizabeth II.

**30 July 2017**

GWR Class 153 No. 368 is seen arriving at Bath Spa coupled up to a GWR Class 150 DMU with a stopping service heading to Gloucester. Of note here is the livery difference of the new GWR green on the 153 and older First Great Western blue on the 150.

**30 November 2022**

GWR Class 158 No. 750 is seen about to depart from Bath Spa with classmate 158749 as they work a long-distance stopping service that runs from Portsmouth Harbour through to Cardiff Central.

**30 November 2022**

GWR Class 158 No. 959 awaits the signal to proceed out of Bath Spa while working the 2C18 from Gloucester through to Frome. The 158s and other DMU fleets are used on a wide variety of stopping services in the local area.

**30 July 2017**

SWT Class 159 No. 106 is seen having just come to a stop at Bath Spa to pick-up and drop-off passengers. This unit is working a stopping service from Waterloo heading to Bristol Temple Meads.

**30 November 2022**

GWR Class 165 No. 126 has just pulled into Bath Spa with classmate 165131 behind as they work towards Bristol Temple Meads with 2V64, which sees the pair heading from Weymouth on the coast through to Gloucester.

**30 July 2017**

Hastings Diesels Class 201 No. 001 is seen at Bath Spa having worked the Strike Back Express railtour, which ran from Hastings to Bath. On this occasion the Hastings set was being lead by DMBS 60118 *Tunbridge Wells*.

**30 November 2022**

GWR Class 800 No. 027 is seen at Bath Spa making a station call along with classmate 800023. The pair make up a ten-car formation that is near journey's end, with the next and final stop being Bristol Temple Meads.

**1 July 2021**

LSL Class 40 No. 013 *Andania* whistles away from Bristol Temple Meads on a fine summer day with the empty coaching stock of the Bristol Forty Railtour, which 40013 worked from Bangor. 013 displays its original number when built; D213 later becoming 40013 when allocated its TOPS number.

**1 July 2021**

GWR Class 43 No. 093 *Old Oak Common HST Depot 1976–2018* is seen arriving at Bristol Temple Meads with a short HST set that is heading from Cardiff to Penzance. When the HST sets were replaced by the IET fleet. Thirty-five Class 43s were retained for working the Cardiff–Penzance route.

**1 July 2021**

GWR Class 43 No. 194 *Okehampton Castle* pulls into Bristol Temple Meads with an unidentified classmate at the rear. When cascaded from GWML and put to work on their new route, the HST sets went from having eight coaches to just four – as can be seen here.

**1 July 2021**

CrossCountry Class 43 No. 285 is seen ticking over while waiting for depature time at Bristol Temple Meads along with classmate 43303, which is out of sight at the other end of this full HST set.

**1 July 2021**

CrossCountry Class 43 No. 366 has just arrived at Bristol Temple Meads along with classmate 43304. The CrossCountry HST sets are used on the routes from the West Country to Edinburgh and Glasgow.

**25 November 2022**

Colas Rail Class 66 No. 849 *Wylam Dilly* is seen on the rear of the local RHTT, working along with classmate 66850 at Bristol Temple Meads on a sunny afternoon. The pair are sitting on the Down through line as they wait to head back to Swindon Transfer.

**25 November 2022**

Colas Rail Class 66 No. 850 *David Maidment OBE* is seen at Bristol Temple Meads along with classmate 66849 as they await the signal to head home on a leaf-busting diagram. The work being done to restore the roof of Temple Meads station is clearly visible in this image.

**25 November 2022**

DRS Class 68s Nos 007 *Valiant* and 001 *Evolution* are seen at Bristol Temple Meads proceeding onto the Up through line, working double-headed with three loaded nuclear flask wagons. The 68s are heading back to the Crewe area with the flasks, which were loaded at Bridgwater and carry spent nuclear fuel for processing.

**July 2021**

GWR Class 158 No. 765 is seen at Bristol Temple Meads waiting its next working along with classmate 158745. The pair are likely going to form a stopping service heading to Exeter St Davids.

**30 November 2022**

GWR Class 158 No. 767 is seen with classmate 158760 as the pair prepare to work the remaining part of diagram 1F14, which runs from Portsmouth Harbour through to Cardiff Central. Due to being a stopping service, the journey takes around three hours.

**1 July 2021**

GWR Class 165 No. 133 is seen at Bristol Temple Meads stabled between duties. Of interest is that 133 is stabled on the old motorail loading point. Vehicles using the service would have entered through the gates and moved on to the loading ramp that is still in place today.

**30 November 2022**

GWR Class 165 No. 128 sits quietly, waiting for any passengers to board before heading out on a local stopping service from Bristol Temple Meads on this cold winter afternoon.

**1 July 2021**

GWR Class 166 No. 214 is seen stabled between duties at Bristol Temple Meads. The Class 166s are used on a variety of services from local stoppers heading to Avonmouth or Severn Beach to longer-distance services to Southampton.

**30 November 2022**

GWR Class 166 No. 215 is about to depart from Bristol Temple Meads with a local stopping service. Note that 215 still carries the previous First Great Western blue livery and might be one of the last to do so as most 166s carry the current GWR green.

**1 July 2021**

CrossCountry Class 220 No. 021 is seen at Bristol Temple Meads with an unidentified Class 220 or 221 waiting to work their next passenger service. The Class 220 and 221 are used on the same routes as the CrossCountry HST sets.

**30 November 2022**

CrossCountry Class 220 No. 033 is seen in tandem with a Class 221 Super Voyager at Bristol Temple Meads as the pair await departure time with a service heading for Plymouth. The arched roof of the main station is visible in the background.

**1 July 2021**

CrossCountry Class 221 No. 124 is seen at Bristol Temple Meads with an unidentified Class 220 or 221 wating to depart on their passenger working. The only difference between the Class 220 and 221 is the number of carriages – the 220 has four and the 221 has five.

**30 November 2022**

GWR Class 802 No. 106 is seen having just arrived at Bristol Temple Meads from London Paddington and is being prepared for its return journey to the capital. 106 carries this very striking Christmas advertising livery for Lilly's Kitchen, which is a pet food company.

**25 November 2022**

Network Rail Stone blower No. DR 80211 is about to enter onto the Up through line at Bristol Temple Meads, where it will wait for the path to proceed. The stone blower was working the 6U31 diagram from Taunton to Severn Tunnel Junction sidings.